The INCREDIBLE OCTOPUS

Meet the Eight-Armed Wonder of the Sea

ERIN SPENCER

Storey Publishing

To Corbin—Every day with you is the adventure of a lifetime.

The mission of Storey Publishing is to serve our customers by
publishing practical information that encourages
personal independence in harmony with the environment.

EDITED BY Hannah Fries
ART DIRECTION AND BOOK DESIGN BY Michaela Jebb
TEXT PRODUCTION BY Jennifer Jepson Smith

COVER PHOTOGRAPHY BY © Blue Planet Archive/Alamy Stock Photo, front c.l. & m.r.; © Jeff Milisen/Alamy Stock Photo, front t.r.; © JonMilnes/Shutterstock, front b.l.; © K A STUDIO/Shutterstock, front c.m.; © Niquirk/Shutterstock, front t.l.; © NOAA/Alamy Stock Photo, front m.l.; © Richard Whitcombe/Shutterstock, front b.r.; © Vittorio Bruno/Shutterstock, back

INTERIOR PHOTOGRAPHY BY © AndamanSE/iStock.com, 33 b., 50; © Avalon.red /Alamy Stock Photo, 47 r.; © B. Murton/Southampton Oceanography Centre /Science Source, 9 t.l.; © Bass Supakit/Shutterstock, 18 b.; © BIOSPHOTO /Alamy Stock Photo, 28 t., 34 t.; © Blue Planet Archive/Alamy Stock Photo, 3 t.l. & b.l., 8 b., 38–39, 63, 68; © Bournemouth News/Shutterstock, 32 b.l.; © British Antarctic Survey/Science Source, 52; Camilla Bowen, 62; © Catherine Withers-Clarke/iStock.com, 30 t.; © Chris Gug/Alamy Stock Photo, 43 r.; Connor Holland /Ocean Image Bank, 12; © DanBrandenburg/iStock.com, 35; © Danita Delimont /Alamy Stock Photo, 18 t.; © Dante Fenolio/Science Source, 49 r.; © David Fleetham/Alamy Stock Photo, 16, 27, 47 t.l., 54–55; David P. Robinson/Ocean Image Bank, 21 t.r.; © David Shale/npl/Minden Pictures, 53 b.; © Dean Pennala /Shutterstock, 21 b.; © DiveIvanov/iStock.com, 20 b.r., 47 m.l.; Dr. John Bruno, 4; © dpa picture alliance/Alamy Stock Photo, 33 m.r.; Edgar Etherington/Public domain/Wikimedia Commons, 57; © fishHook Photography/Alamy Stock Photo, 60; © Fotokon/Shutterstock, 8 r.; © FrankStratton/iStock.com, 11 b.; © Fred Bavendam/Minden Pictures, 19 t., 28 b., 49 b.l.; © FtLaudGirl /iStock.com, 41 b.; © Gerald Robert Fischer/Shutterstock, 42 b.; © Gialdini Luca /Shutterstock, 24 t.r.; Grant Thomas/Ocean Image Bank, 9 b.r.; © Howard Chew/Alamy Stock Photo, 24 t.l.; Jayne Jenkins/Ocean Image Bank, 41 t.; © Jeff Milisen/Alamy Stock Photo, 3 b.r.; © Jeff Rotman/Alamy Stock Photo, 49 t.l., 51; © Joao.Carraro/Shutterstock, 15 b.r.; © joebelanger/iStock.com, 29 l.; © John Dambik/Alamy Stock Photo, 53 t.; © John Lewis/Auscape /Minden Pictures, 19 b.r.; © Jonpaul Hosking/Shutterstock, 30 b.; © K A STUDIO /Shutterstock, 5; Lewis Burnett/Ocean Image Bank, 13; © Mark Kirkland /VWPics/Alamy Stock Photo, 9 t.r.; © maskalin/iStock.com, 6; © Megan Cook, 59 t.r.; © NOAA/Alamy Stock Photo, 8 l., 44 t.l. & b.; © Norbert Wu/Minden Pictures, 9 b.l.; Ocean Exploration Trust and NOAA ONMS, 59 b.r.; Ocean Exploration Trust/Institute for Exploration/CC BY-SA 3.0/Wikimedia Commons, 58; © Petr Slezak/Shutterstock, 31; © R. de Bruijn_Photography/Shutterstock, 48; © randimal/iStock.com, 9 c.; © REUTERS/Alamy Stock Photo, 32 b.m.; © Richard Whitcombe/Shutterstock, 1; © Roman Vintonyak/Shutterstock, 30 m.; © Sam Robertshaw/Shutterstock, 42 t.; © Sascha Janson/Shutterstock, 24 b.l.; © scubaluna/iStock.com, 20 t.r.; © SergeUWPhoto/Shutterstock, 41 t. (inset); © Sergey Popov V/Shutterstock, 11 t.; © Shane Gross/naturepl.com, 33 t.; © Shpatak/Shutterstock, 14–15; © Solvin Zankl/naturepl.com, 43 l.; © Solvin Zankl/npl//Minden Pictures, 45; © Subaqueosshutterbug/iStock.com, 25, 40; © Thierry Eidenweil/Shutterstock, 32 t.r.; Tommaso Ranzani, 65; Tracey Jennings/Ocean Image Bank, 21 t.l.; © Trueog/iStock.com, 46 b.; © Velvetfish /iStock.com, 47 b.l.; © Vitalii Kalutskyi/iStock.com, 24 b.r.; © Vittorio Bruno /Shutterstock, 22–23; © WaterFrame/Alamy Stock Photo, 46 t.l.; © Whitepointer /iStock.com, 20 l.; © Yusuke Yoshino/Nature Production/Minden Pictures, 29 r.; Courtesy of Z Yan Wang, 61; © ZUMA Press Inc/Alamy Stock Photo, 34 b.

ILLUSTRATIONS BY © Katie Melrose

TEXT © 2024 by Erin T. Spencer

Storey books may be purchased in bulk for business, educational, or promotional use. Special editions or book excerpts can also be created to specification. For details, please contact your local bookseller or the Hachette Book Group Special Markets Department at special.markets@hbgusa.com.

Storey Publishing
210 MASS MoCA Way
North Adams, MA 01247
storey.com

Storey Publishing is an imprint of Workman Publishing, a division of Hachette Book Group, Inc., 1290 Avenue of the Americas, New York, NY 10104.

Distributed in Europe by Hachette Livre, 58 rue Jean Bleuzen, 92 178 Vanves Cedex, France
Distributed in the United Kingdom by Hachette Book Group, UK, Carmelite House, 50 Victoria Embankment, London EC4Y 0DZ

ISBNs: 978-1-63586-628-5 (Paper Over Board); 978-1-63586-629-2 (Fixed Format EPUB); 978-1-63586-837-1 (Fixed Format PDF); 978-1-63586-838-8 (Fixed Format Kindle)

Printed in China through Asia Pacific Offset on paper from responsible sources
10 9 8 7 6 5 4 3 2 1

Library of Congress Cataloging-in-Publication Data on file

Contents

The Cool and Creative OCTOPUS

OCTOPUSES ARE SUCH FASCINATING CREATURES, it's hard to know where to begin. With their eight bendy arms, color-changing skin, and incredible brains, they are truly unlike any other animal on the planet!

Let's investigate what makes the octopus so special. Together, we will learn about this weird and amazing animal, exploring questions like:

Are there octopuses in the deep sea?

Why do octopuses use ink?

How do octopuses change color?

What does an octopus researcher do?

How can I help octopuses?

. . . and more!

So buckle up your scuba gear. It's going to be a wild ride!

—*Erin Spencer*
Marine Biologist

DID YOU KNOW?

The name *octopus* comes from the Greek word meaning *"EIGHT FEET"*!

There are about *300 SPECIES* of octopus living in oceans all over the world!

Octopuses can *CHANGE COLOR!*
(page 25)

Octopuses have **THREE HEARTS!** (page 12)

Octopuses are some of the **SMARTEST** animals on the planet! (page 32)

Octopuses like to **PLAY WITH TOYS!** (page 34)

The largest giant Pacific octopus ever found was **30 FEET LONG!** (page 48)

There are octopuses in **ANTARCTICA!** (page 52)

Octopuses have **BLUE BLOOD!**

The blue-ringed octopus is one of the **MOST VENOMOUS** animals on Earth! (page 40)

All About
OCTOPUSES

Eight-armed biology, from head to sucker

Where Do Octopuses Live?

More like, where *don't* octopuses live!? Octopuses are found in every part of the ocean, from the tropics to Antarctica and from the shallows to the deep sea.

DEEP SEA. The deep sea is cold, dark, and under a lot of pressure—not ideal for most animals. However, some animals thrive here. Deep-sea octopuses like the dumbo octopus can live thousands of feet below the surface (see page 44).

OPEN OCEAN. The argonaut, also known as the paper nautilus, lives in the open ocean. This creature uses its unique shell to trap air and float along the surface (see page 42).

TROPICS. Many octopuses, including the common octopus, are found in tropical waters near the equator.

HYDROTHERMAL VENTS. These deep-sea **habitats** are toxic to most animals but home to others, including some octopuses.

KELP FORESTS. Made of huge, swaying plants called kelp, this habitat is the perfect hiding spot for many animals, including octopuses. Young red octopuses like to hang out near kelp by the seafloor.

TIDE POOLS. Sometimes you can spot an octopus in a rocky tide pool, searching for its next meal!

ANTARCTICA. For some octopuses, the cold never bothered them anyway! Antarctica is home to a few octopus species that are specially adapted to cold temperatures (see page 52).

CORAL REEFS. Reefs have lots of food and shelter for octopuses to explore. What's not to love?

Invertebrates Rule

What do dolphins, elephants, dogs, birds, and humans have in common? They all have backbones!

Animals can be split into two groups: **vertebrates**, or animals with backbones, and **invertebrates**, or animals without backbones. Stretch up to the sky—can you feel your backbone? Our bones help us grow big and tall, and they protect our sensitive insides, like our heart and lungs. However, animals without bones far outnumber animals that have them. In fact, 97 percent of animals on Earth are invertebrates!

There are a lot of different types of invertebrates, including crabs, insects, corals, slugs, and oysters. Octopuses are part of a group of invertebrates called **mollusks**. Most mollusks, like clams and snails, have soft bodies protected by hard outer shells.

Cephalopods

Octopuses and their relatives are a *little* bit different from other mollusks. They are part of an even smaller group called **cephalopods** (SEF-uh-la-pods). Their name means "head foot" because their heads are connected directly to their "legs" (which are actually called "arms").

There are four types of cephalopods: octopus, **squid**, **cuttlefish**, and **nautilus**. Of these four, only nautiluses have outer shells.

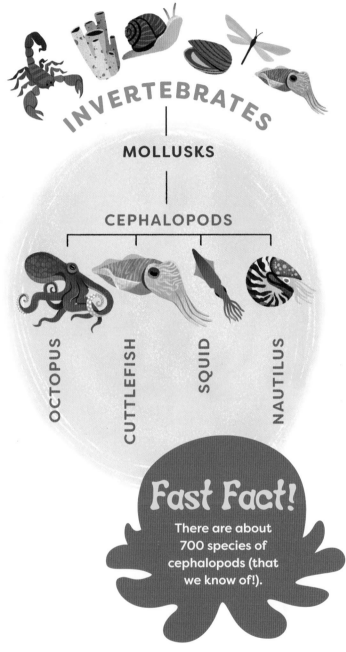

INVERTEBRATES

MOLLUSKS

CEPHALOPODS

OCTOPUS   CUTTLEFISH   SQUID   NAUTILUS

Fast Fact!

There are about 700 species of cephalopods (that we know of!).

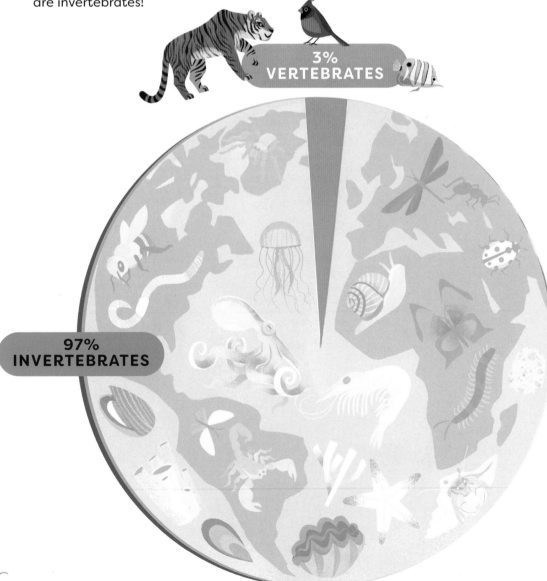

3%
VERTEBRATES

97%
INVERTEBRATES

This octopus has **FOLDED ITSELF** inside a small jar.

Octopi vs. Octopuses

What happens when you have more than one octopus? Although you might have heard them referred to as *octopi*, the correct term is *octopuses*, just like how *bus* becomes *buses*.

ANATOMY OF AN OCTOPUS

HEARTS. Octopuses have three hearts. They use two to pump blood to the gills and one to pump blood to the rest of the body. Octopus blood is blue!

MANTLE. This muscular sac holds all of an octopus's organs, including the hearts and gills.

Stomach

Ink sac

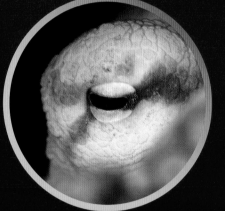

EYES. Octopus eyes are pretty similar to ours. They can sense light but don't see colors the way we do.

SIPHON. This is a hollow tube used for movement. Octopuses can pull water through their mantle and blow it out the siphon to propel themselves along.

WEB. The arms are connected by stretches of skin called webs. The thickness and length of the webs varies among species.

BRAIN. Octopuses have one big main brain situated behind the eyes and eight "mini brains," one in each arm. Learn more about how this system works on page 16.

Arms vs. Tentacles

Octopuses have arms, not tentacles! Arms are covered with suckers all along their bottom, but tentacles have suckers only at the very tip. You can find tentacles on other cephalopods like cuttlefish and squid.

ARMS. Octopuses have eight bendy arms (not tentacles!) that help them sense their environment, move around, and capture **prey**.

SUCKERS. These are not your average suction cups. Each sucker can move separately from the others and can "taste" the world around it. Learn more about suckers on page 15.

BEAK. Beaks aren't only for birds! Octopus beaks are very sharp and look like parrot beaks. They help octopuses break down their food and even inject venom.

RADULA. Imagine if your tongue were covered with teeth—pretty creepy! A radula is like a long strip with rows of teeth that help octopuses eat their prey.

MOUTH. The octopus's mouth is at the center of its underside, where its arms meet.

Suckers!

There are so many things to love about octopuses, but they might be best known for their **suckers**. Can you picture an octopus without them? It would be weird, right?

Suckers are some of the best tools in an octopus's toolbox. They help the octopus move, taste, and lock itself in place.

Different species of octopus have different numbers and patterns of suckers. For example, the giant Pacific octopus has 280 suckers *on each arm*. That means that one giant Pacific octopus has more than 2,200 suckers! (See page 48 for more about giant Pacific octopuses.) Meanwhile, a smaller Antarctic octopus tends to have only about 50 suckers per arm (see page 52). Studying the suckers is one way scientists can ID species they don't recognize.

Sucker Facts

Although suckers look like the typical suction cup you might see somewhere at home, they are extra special. Check it out.

- **OCTOPUS SUCKERS CAN FOLD AND BEND** to fit all kinds of surfaces, from smooth glass to bumpy rocks.

- **SUCKERS NOT ONLY FEEL OBJECTS BUT CAN "TASTE" THEM, TOO!** They also have a bunch of **nerves** so they can send lots of information to the brain.

- **EACH SUCKER CAN MOVE ON ITS OWN,** independent of the other suckers. That means the octopus can move small things from sucker to sucker without ever moving an arm. It's like a tiny assembly line of suckers, all working to make an octopus's life easier.

- **OCTOPUSES CAN SOLVE MAZES** with their arms, even if they can't see the maze with their eyes! They use the sensors in their suckers to feel their way along.

Fast Fact!

Why don't octopuses get stuck on their own suckers? Octopus skin sends a special chemical signal that tells the suckers, "Don't stick!"

UNDER A MICROSCOPE, you can see teeny-tiny grooves around a sucker's edge and teeny-tiny hairs at the bottom. These make the sucker's grip *extra* strong.

THIS OCTOPUS IS EATING A MUSSEL. Just by touching it, the octopus can sense it's not a rock—it's a mussel. Yum! By attaching its suckers to the shell with a vacuum seal, the octopus gets a tight grip. Then it uses its strong arm muscles to pull the two halves of the shell apart.

Nine Brains??

Our **nervous system** makes everything we do possible, from walking to breathing to reading this book. In humans, the nervous system is made up of a brain, a spinal cord that runs all the way down our backbone, and a series of nerves. Nerves are like little wires that carry information around our brain and body using tiny messengers called **neurons**.

Almost every animal you can think of has a nervous system, including fish, dogs, insects, and even jellyfish. Not all animal nervous systems look like ours do (for example, jellyfish don't have brains), but they are all responsible for sending messages. Cephalopods have a very unusual nervous system—and the largest one of any invertebrate.

Octopuses have almost as many neurons as dogs do— about half a billion.

Like us, octopuses have a brain that directs the rest of the body. The octopus's brain is in the mantle, or the central part of its body (see page 12). Most octopus neurons are not in their brains, though. Instead, two-thirds of their neurons are in their arms and skin! In fact, each of an octopus's eight arms has its own "mini brain."

Although an octopus's central brain calls most of the shots, each arm can practically think for itself. Each arm can touch, smell, and taste its way through the world. Meanwhile, the central brain keeps sending instructions to the arms' mini brains.

Growing a New Arm

Octopus arms can move even if they're cut off! Thanks to their many neurons, detached arms can still feel around and even grab for food. Plus, losing an arm is no big deal for the octopus because it can regenerate, or grow back, a lost arm. The process might take a few months, but after a while the octopus will have eight arms once again.

The tip of this octopus's arm is starting to grow back.

CENTRAL BRAIN

"MINI BRAIN"
One in each arm!

CAN YOU IMAGINE
if your arms and legs had
their own brains? They
would have minds of
their own—literally!

Octopus Babies!

When it comes to **reproduction**, octopuses once again have a unique approach.

It takes both a male and a female octopus to make baby octopuses, which start out as eggs. The female is the one in charge of making sure those eggs grow into healthy baby octopuses. As a matter of fact, the male's job is done before the female even lays her eggs! After they mate, the male octopus dies. Then the female waits until conditions are just right before she lays her eggs.

Once the momma finds a good place to settle down, like in a cave or under a rock, she will lay her eggs in clusters connected by a thin string. They kind of look like bunches of grapes!

Babies Adrift

As the eggs develop, the momma octopus will not move. She won't even leave to eat! As long as no **predator** bothers her, she will spend 24 hours a day blowing water over the eggs and picking away algae. This keeps the eggs clean and healthy.

It takes months before the eggs are ready to hatch. When the time comes, the baby octopuses will break out of their eggs and drift into the world. The babies are on their own once they start this journey because mother octopuses die right around the time the eggs hatch.

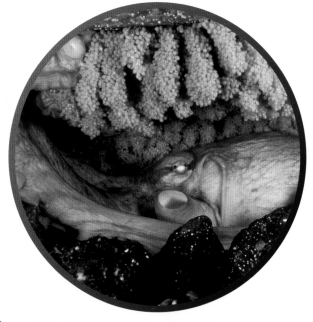

THE GIANT PACIFIC OCTOPUS can lay up to 100,000 eggs that hang in bunches.

Fast Fact!

Sometimes male and female octopuses are very different sizes. For example, female blanket octopuses are 40,000 times heavier than males!

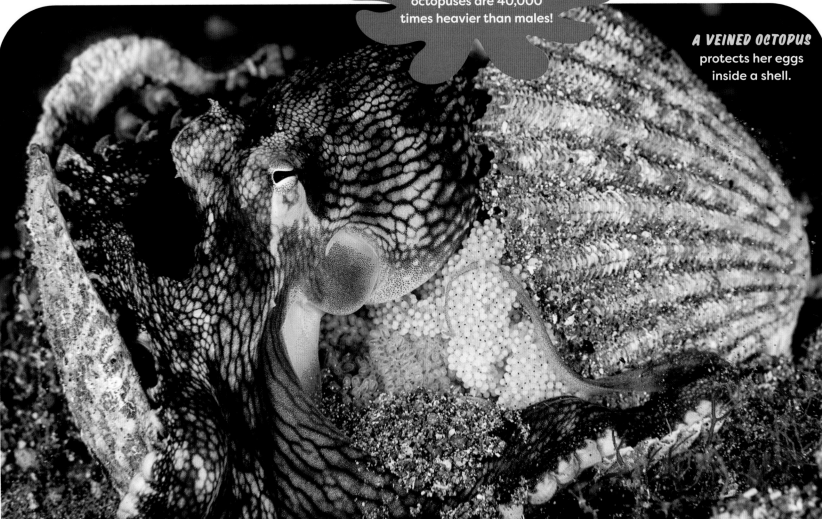

A VEINED OCTOPUS protects her eggs inside a shell.

MOST BABIES are too little to swim on their own, so they rely on ocean currents to move them around. Eventually they grow big enough to sink to the bottom and start their life along the seafloor.

You can see the TINY OCTOPUSES inside these eggs!

A southern sand octopus is hatching from its egg.

Different Octopuses, Different Plans

Not all octopuses reproduce the same way. Momma argonauts, for example, are unique in that they have a thin shell in which they carry their eggs (see page 42). Scientists also discovered one deep-sea octopus that had an even *more* extreme approach: She stayed by her eggs, likely without eating, for four and a half years!

Octopus Relatives

Squid, cuttlefish, and nautiluses are cephalopods, too. Like octopuses, squid and cuttlefish have soft bodies and eight arms. Unlike octopuses, they also have two tentacles. You can tell the difference between arms and tentacles by looking at their suckers: Tentacles are a little longer than arms and have suckers piled up at the tip, rather than along the entire underside.

SQUID have long, torpedo-like bodies. They are fast predators and can travel long distances.

CUTTLEFISH are shorter and broader and typically move more slowly than squid. One easy way you can tell squid and cuttlefish apart? Look at their eyes! Squid have a round eye center, but cuttlefish have a W-shaped center.

NAUTILUSES are quite different from octopuses, squid, and cuttlefish. They don't have any arms at all—only tentacles! Although squid and cuttlefish have tentacles, too, nautiluses take it to another level. They have more than 90 tentacles that they use to capture their prey. Their tentacles don't have any suckers.

▼ Striped pyjama squid look ready for Halloween. And they are actually cuttlefish! They hang out near the ocean bottom and even "walk" along the seafloor.

▼ Flamboyant cuttlefish use their chromatophores (see page 25) to flash bright yellow, purple, white, and red when startled by a predator.

Fast Fact!
The longest cephalopod on the planet is the giant squid, which can stretch to 55 feet!

NAUTILUSES are the only cephalopods with an outer shell.

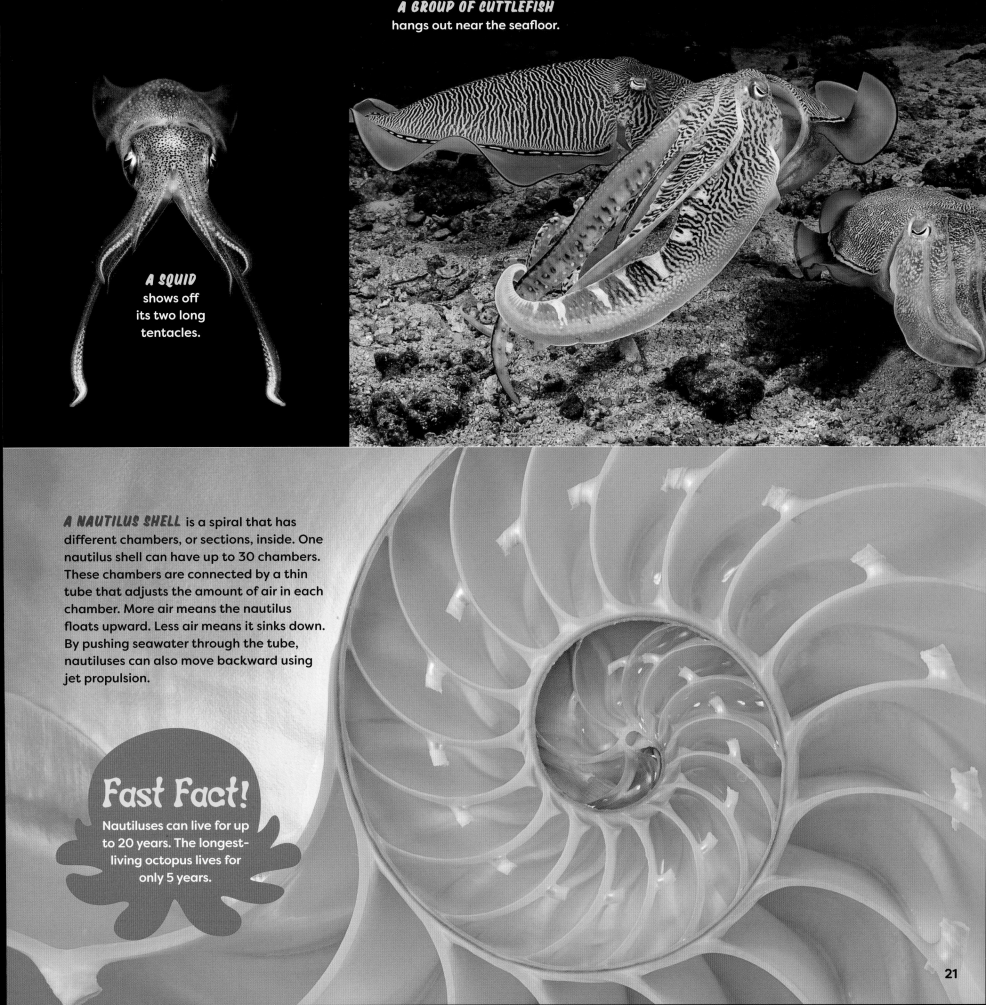

A SQUID
shows off
its two long
tentacles.

A NAUTILUS SHELL is a spiral that has different chambers, or sections, inside. One nautilus shell can have up to 30 chambers. These chambers are connected by a thin tube that adjusts the amount of air in each chamber. More air means the nautilus floats upward. Less air means it sinks down. By pushing seawater through the tube, nautiluses can also move backward using jet propulsion.

Fast Fact!

Nautiluses can live for up to 20 years. The longest-living octopus lives for only 5 years.

The OCTOPUS LIFE

Brains, brawn, and survival strategies

CAN YOU SEE the octopuses in these photos?

Now You See Me . . .

One of the octopus's coolest superpowers is its ability to change color. Octopuses often use this superpower to **camouflage** themselves to match their surroundings so that it's harder for predators to find them. Imagine being able to blend into your couch or the wall behind you—it would be the ultimate game of hide-and-seek!

So How Do They Do It?

The secret to octopus camouflage lies in their skin. Octopuses have **chromatophores**—tiny bags of color that grow or shrink based on signals around them. Picture holding a white balloon filled with red paint. When you pinch the lip of the balloon closed, you just see a white ball. But when you stretch the lip open wide, you can see the red color peeking up from the bottom of the balloon. The wider you stretch the lip, the more color you see.

Chromatophores work kind of the same way! The sacs of **pigment**, or color, are surrounded by small muscles. When the muscles tighten, the sacs stretch open and reveal the color inside.

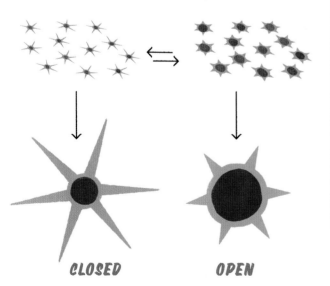

CLOSED   OPEN

Most octopuses have red, yellow, brown, or black pigments, and they can mix and match them to show a range of colors. For example, they can be brownish yellow against a sandy bottom, then swap to a dark gray while sitting on a rock. They can even make stripes or spots or change each half of their body to a different color!

Shape-Shifters

Octopuses can change shape, too! They have skin bumps called **papillae**, which they can use to match the bumpiness of coral or rock. They can be smooth one minute and bumpy the next, all depending on their surroundings. See an example of another type of shape-shifter, the mimic octopus, on page 46.

Fast Fact!
Octopuses can change color in less than one-tenth of a second. If you blink, you'll miss it!

Going Shiny
Some species take the color show to the next level with **iridophores**, iridescent chromatophores that reflect light like little mirrors. Iridophores make the shimmery rings that the blue-ringed octopus is known for (see page 40).

You've Been Inked!

Without a hard shell or sharp claws to protect themselves, octopuses need plenty of other strategies to escape stressful situations. In addition to their cleverness, camouflage, and shape-shifting superpowers, many octopuses use ink to confuse predators.

Octopus ink looks similar to the ink in a fountain pen, but it gets its coloring from a pigment called **melanin**. Lots of animals have melanin in their bodies, including us! In humans, melanin creates the color in skin, eyes, and hair. Melanin makes octopus ink very dark and difficult to see through.

If a predator gets too close, an octopus can spew out a blob of ink, which is stored in an ink sac inside its body. This makes it hard for the predator to see, giving the octopus time to swim away. The octopus can also squeeze out ink in a long, thin line, which some scientists think might look to a predator like a stinging tentacle.

As if all that wasn't enough, octopus ink contains a substance that irritates predators' eyes and messes up their sense of smell. Plus, ink with a lot of mucus could clog fish gills, making it harder for them to breathe. Pretty handy, right?

Fast Fact!

People in ancient times used cephalopod ink to write with!

Sometimes octopuses add *THICK MUCUS* to the ink so that it hangs together in the water, creating an octopus-shaped blob to confuse a predator!

Ink's Not for Everyone

Not all octopuses have ink. It isn't so useful in the deep sea, where it would blend into the already dark, dark waters. Octopuses who hunt at night don't use it either.

27

What Do Octopuses Eat?

What makes up an octopus's meal depends on many things, including the octopus's size, the amount of food available, how nutritious the food is, and more. It can be a lot of work for an octopus to find, capture, and eat its prey. Generally, octopuses try to find the most satisfying meal that takes the least amount of work. If you've ever poked around the kitchen looking for a snack, you can probably relate!

Octopuses are carnivores, meaning they eat other animals. The menu can include snails, sea slugs, clams, crabs, fish, and sometimes other octopuses.

How an Octopus Prepares Its Dinner

Here are a few techniques octopuses use to get their meals.

DRILL! Sometimes animal shells are really strong and difficult for an octopus to pull apart. The octopus can use its radula, or band of teeth, to drill a hole right through the shell to the soft prey inside.

BREAK! An octopus's beak is hard and strong. It can *chip chip chip* away at a shell with its beak until the shell breaks apart.

MELT! Why break it when you can dissolve it? Some octopuses use acid to melt away part of a shell so they can grab the prey inside.

PARALYZE! Octopuses can inject their prey with a venom that makes it stop moving (and easier to eat).

PULL! With their strong arms and tight suckers, octopuses can get a really good grip. By attaching their arms to opposite sides of a closed shell, they can pull the halves apart.

An octopus eats a crab.

Giant Pacific octopuses sometimes *EAT SHARKS* (like this one) or even unlucky birds.

An octopus **PULLS APART A SHELL** to get at the meat inside.

Menu Clues

Scientists can see what animals eat by observing them in the wild or looking at what's inside their stomachs. Some octopuses make it even easier to figure out their menu: After eating their prey, they'll toss the shell outside their den in a pile called a midden. By looking at the thrown-out shells, scientists can tell what the octopus ate and how they ate it.

A common octopus **HIDES** in a hollow brick, surrounded by its midden of shells.

What Eats Octopuses?

Animals like sharks, eels, dolphins, seals, orcas, and seabirds all munch on octopuses. In fact, at first glance, octopuses seem like a perfect meal! They don't have pesky shells or spines, and most aren't poisonous. They're soft, full of protein, and found throughout the world.

Octopuses can be a major source of food for some animals but just an occasional snack for others. For example, a nurse shark that lives on a reef might eat a lot of octopuses, while a seagull might eat one only if the octopus is stranded in a tide pool.

On the Defense

Because they lack physical protection, octopuses have to use their smarts and trickery to bamboozle and escape from predators. The easiest way to avoid getting eaten is to not be seen in the first place! Octopuses can use camouflage to blend into their surroundings and hide (see page 25). If spotted, they can puff themselves up to look big and scary, change colors to confuse the predator, or squeeze into small, hard-to-reach crevices. If that doesn't work, they can spew ink to confuse the predators and jet away (see page 26).

If they do end up getting caught, they don't make it easy on their predators. A study in Australia saw dolphins shaking and even tossing octopuses in the air before eating them. Researchers suspect it's because octopuses are tough to handle and can even choke dolphins with their arms.

Although it might be weird to think about animals eating octopuses, it's all part of a healthy **ecosystem**. Sometimes the predator might win. Other times a predator is left hungry because of a quick-thinking octopus.

A seal eats an octopus.

Whitetip reef sharks prey on octopuses as well.

A moray eel would be happy to have an octopus meal.

A study in Alaska's Beaufort Sea found that octopuses make up about half of a beluga whale's diet in springtime. One whale had almost *150 OCTOPUSES IN ITS STOMACH*— now that's a big meal!

Octopuses Are Smart

What does it mean to be smart? When we think of a "smart person," we might picture someone who is really good at math problems or puzzles. But there is so much more to being smart!

With animals, scientists define **intelligence** as an animal's ability to solve problems by learning about its environment. The animal kingdom is full of clever critters. Most of the animals we think of as intelligent—like chimpanzees, dolphins, crows, and elephants—are vertebrates. But animals with backbones aren't the only smarty-pants! Cephalopods, including octopuses, are the smartest invertebrates on the planet. The more we study them, the more they show us how much they can learn and remember.

Brainpower

To study octopus sea smarts, let's start with their brain. They have the largest brain compared to their body size of any invertebrate. They spend a lot of time growing that big, complex brain, which they use to explore the world around them and make choices that help them get food and avoid being eaten. (Did you know octopuses actually have eight "mini brains" in addition to their main brain? See page 16 to learn more.)

SOME COOL WAYS OCTOPUSES USE THEIR BRAINS

How many of these things do *you* do, too?

THEY SOLVE PUZZLES. Though they may not be able to solve Rubik's cubes, octopuses do solve other puzzles that aquarium staff give them to keep them entertained. Sometimes there's even a treat inside!

This octopus is opening a jar to get at some tasty snacks at a zoo.

THEY OPEN JARS. Using their suckers and arms, octopuses can twist open lids—even when the octopus is inside the jar! The fastest octopuses can pop the top in less than a minute.

THEY SHOW PERSONALITIES. Scientists and aquariums have seen that octopuses have different personalities, just like people do. Some are bold and come up to people right away. Others can be shy and hide in their tanks.

THEY PLAY WITH TOYS.
There are many stories of octopuses playing with Legos, empty bottles, and even Mr. Potato Head! Play is a sign of intelligence. Turn the page to learn more!

An octopus holds a toilet brush used to clean its tank.

An octopus uses a shell as a tool for hiding.

THEY FINISH MAZES. Scientists found that octopuses can learn how to solve mazes. Even if they can't see the maze with their eyes, they can use the sensors in their suckers to feel their way along.

THEY RECOGNIZE PEOPLE.
Some octopuses can tell two people apart by their faces, even when they are wearing the same clothes!

THEY USE TOOLS. We know animals like crows and chimps use tools. Octopuses do, too, which is unusual for invertebrates! Some octopuses carry around shells to hide in when a predator is nearby.

Let's Play!

Have you ever played fetch with a dog? Think about how they jump around, wag their tail, and chase after a ball—they're having fun! When animals play, it helps them relieve stress, build friendships, and practice skills.

Scientists have done experiments to see how octopuses play. In one, they gave octopuses Legos. After feeling the Legos with their suckers to make sure they weren't food, the octopuses started to play. They dragged the toys across the surface of the water, pushed and pulled them, and passed them between their arms (kind of like playing catch!). Other researchers have seen an octopus play by jetting water at an empty bottle to push it away, waiting for it to drift back, then jetting water at it again.

Why do octopuses play? We don't really know, but scientists think it's a way to keep their brains busy when they're bored. That's why aquariums make sure to give their octopuses lots of things to do to keep them happy and healthy!

One octopus liked its Mr. Potato Head so much, it wouldn't let anyone take the toy away from it!

Is this food? Or is it a toy? This octopus is using its suckers to investigate *A RUBBER DUCK.*

How Can We Tell If an Animal Is Playing?

Since animals can't tell us themselves, scientists have come up with a list. For an action to be considered play, all of the following things need to be true:

- It happens when the animal is relaxed.

- It doesn't help the animal get food, shelter, or other basic needs.

- It is different from the animal's normal behavior.

- It happens over and over again.

- It is fun!

Think about when you play a game— do these things describe human play, too?

OCTOPUSES WHO BROKE THE RULES

With their ability to shape-shift and squeeze through tiny holes and crevices, it's no surprise that octopuses have found themselves in some sticky situations. Here are some famous octopus antics.

Octo Flood

A female California two-spot octopus tinkered with part of the water pipe near its tank at the Heal the Bay Aquarium in Santa Monica. Hundreds of gallons of salt water poured over the floors, flooding the aquarium and causing a big headache for the people who had to clean it up!

Inky Goes Home

In one of the most famous octopus adventures, Inky the octopus escaped its tank at the National Aquarium of New Zealand. Inky snuck out of a small hole in its tank, crawled across the floor, and squeezed down a drain to the sea.

Lights Out

In Germany, Otto the octopus kept squirting water at the lights near its tank, causing them to go out. The staff at the Sea Star Aquarium couldn't figure out what was happening until they stayed overnight in the aquarium and caught Otto in the act.

Stealing Snacks

Lumpfish kept disappearing from an aquarium in Brighton, England. Every day people would show up to find fewer and fewer fish in the tank! Eventually they found the culprit: An octopus had been crawling out of its tank and into the lumpfish tank for a snack.

Fast Fact!

Some octopuses are sneakier than others! One study found that the giant Pacific octopus and the common octopus were more likely to escape their tanks than other species.

Is Escaping a Good Thing?

Although it might seem like octopuses are "trying to escape" (like in *Finding Nemo*), they probably do these things because they are naturally curious and used to leaving their dens to look for food.

In fact, climbing out of their tank can be dangerous for octopuses. They can't survive out of water for long and may run into chemicals or other threats that could make them sick—or worse.

When it comes to keeping octopuses in aquariums, leave it to the pros! They know what it takes to keep octopuses happy, healthy, and safe in their enclosures.

Meet the
OCTOPUSES

From smallest to largest, deepest to coldest

MOST VENOMOUS
Blue-Ringed Octopus

WHAT IS THE SIZE OF A GOLF BALL, is covered in spots, and can kill you? The blue-ringed octopus.

Blue-ringed octopuses like to hang out in shallow seagrass beds or sandy-bottom reefs and snack on small crabs and shrimp. To paralyze their prey, they produce **tetrodotoxin,** a toxin that is up to 100 times more deadly than black widow spider venom.

This toxin is also very handy for defending against predators. If it feels threatened, the octopus flashes its bright, shimmery blue rings to warn predators to STAY AWAY. The octopus injects the toxin through a tiny but dangerous bite. Even if a predator manages to eat an octopus without being bitten, the toxin will still make them sick (though that's less dangerous than being bitten).

Fortunately, blue-ringed octopuses aren't typically aggressive—they would rather you just leave them alone!

RUNNER-UP
It's a Tie!

Believe it or not, all octopuses are venomous! However, only the blue-ringed octopus is dangerous to humans. Other octopuses use their venom mainly to paralyze their prey.

Fast Fact!

Blue-ringed octopuses have a painless bite, but it can kill an adult human in minutes!

AUTHOR'S NOTE:
These are my favorite octopuses! Shhhh, don't tell the others.

When the blue-ringed octopus is relaxed, it uses its camouflage to blend into the sandy bottom around reefs.

Hands Off!

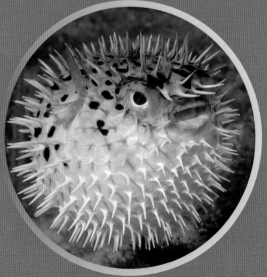

Blue-ringed octopuses aren't the only ones who have tetrodotoxin. Some starfish, snails, and worms have it, too. Even pufferfish have the toxin, but people can still eat pufferfish if they're prepared really, *really* carefully. Definitely not something to try at home.

On land, some newts and frogs have tetrodotoxin as well. Why do so many different types of species have the same toxin? Scientists think that rather than make the toxin themselves, animals get it from bacteria. They either absorb the bacteria or eat food that has the bacteria in it. Then these critters keep the toxin for themselves to use against predators or to capture prey!

MOST INVENTIVE
Argonaut

OCTOPUSES USE A LOT OF STRANGE TECHNIQUES to survive and thrive in the ocean. But the argonaut is truly unique.

Argonauts don't look like other octopuses. That's because they have "shells" that look like the ones nautiluses make. Unlike nautilus shells, argonaut shells are very thin, almost like paper. This cool feature inspired their nickname, the "paper nautilus." Each argonaut shell is unique, like a snowflake, with slightly different colors and patterns. No other octopus has anything like it!

Many octopus species lay their eggs in protected dens on the seafloor (see page 18). Not argonauts! Argonauts are pelagic, meaning they live in the open ocean. They prefer to take their babies on the go. Females lay their eggs inside their protective shell and keep drifting along, through warm tropical and subtropical waters, until the eggs hatch.

Argonauts' shells also help them float! The argonauts grab air bubbles at the surface and keep them in their shells to stay buoyant.

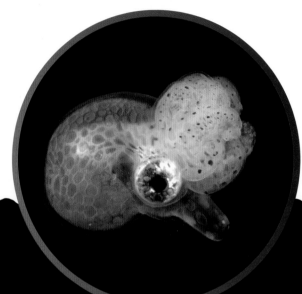

A BABY ARGONAUT shows the beginnings of a thin shell.

Argonaut Fact or Fiction?

For a while, scientists thought argonauts took their shells from other animals rather than build them themselves. They also thought that argonauts used their arms to catch the breeze at the ocean surface, like sails on a sailboat. Although that sounds really cool, it's not true. But the truth about argonauts is cool enough!

Fast Fact!

Since they don't have eggs to take care of, male argonauts don't get to enjoy a shell. They are much smaller than the females—only about one-tenth their size! That would be like an action figure standing next to the real superhero. A big difference, right?

RUNNER-UP
Blanket Octopus

Although they don't have shells, blanket octopuses do have big "blankets" of skin connecting their arms that make them look bigger to potential predators. They have another cool trick, too: Young blanket octopuses steal stinging tentacles from other ocean critters to protect themselves against predators.

DEEPEST
Dumbo Octopus

IF YOU DOVE DOWN, DOWN, DOWN to the deep sea, you'd find a completely different world. It looks more like the surface of the moon than the colorful coral reefs and swaying kelp forests of the sunlit zone! Deep under all that water, the world is dark, cold, and under a huge amount of pressure.

Nevertheless, plenty of animals call the deep sea home, including the dumbo octopus, the deepest-dwelling octopus we know. Dumbo octopuses have been spotted more than 20,000 feet below the surface, in the **hadal zone**, which is the deepest zone in the ocean.

Scientists have found fewer than 20 species of dumbo octopus—so far. Because the deep sea is so hard to get to, there is a lot we still don't know about the animals who live there, including octopuses. Most of what we know about dumbo octopuses comes from looking at specimens in museums or images made by special cameras that can handle the pressure of the deep sea.

CAN YOU GUESS HOW the dumbo octopus got its name? The two fins on top of the mantle look like Dumbo the elephant's ears. The octopus uses the fins to move through the water instead of relying on its siphon, like many other octopuses do.

Why Is Life So Hard in the Deep Sea?

Not many animals can handle the intense environment of the deep sea. Those that do have special adaptations to help them survive. What makes it so tough to get by?

- **THEY'RE UNDER A LOT OF PRESSURE—LITERALLY.** In the deepest parts of the ocean, the pressure is more than 1,000 times greater than it is on the surface. Our bones could never stand the pressure of the deep sea. That's one reason you'll find only invertebrates there!

- **IT IS *REALLY* CHILLY** in the deep sea. Temperatures are close to freezing. Some animals deal with the cold by making special antifreeze proteins in their bodies.

- **IT IS INCREDIBLY DARK.** Sunlight doesn't make it down to the deep sea, so the only light comes from animals who can make their own light, called **bioluminescence**.

RUNNER-UP
Glass Octopus

A few other types of octopuses also call the deep sea home, but glass octopuses are one of the flashiest. They are practically clear (like glass, get it?), so you can see straight through their bodies to their internal organs. They can live 3,000 feet below the surface and grow to almost 2 feet long.

WANT TO LEARN MORE about what it's like to study the deep sea? See page 59!

BEST DISGUISED
Mimic Octopus

IT'S A FISH! IT'S A SNAKE! It's . . . an octopus pretending to be a fish and a snake?

The mimic octopus is truly a master of disguise. There are few better tricksters in the animal kingdom.

Mimic octopuses live in sandy and muddy habitats in the Indian and Pacific Oceans. They are covered in brown-and-white stripes and have spindly arms that can grow to two feet in length. By moving their arms in unusual ways, they can take on the appearance of other sea critters. They're extra special because they can copy other animals' looks *and* actions.

Scientists still have a lot to learn about these copycats, but researchers suspect mimic octopuses imitate toxic animals to warn predators to stay away. They also think these octopuses may have even more disguises that we don't know about yet.

WHAT OTHER OCEAN ANIMALS do you think the mimic octopus could look like?

ALTER EGOS OF THE MIMIC OCTOPUS

SEA SNAKE

The mimic octopus can hide six of its arms, then stretch the remaining two out wide to look like a venomous sea snake. They do this when threatened by pushy damselfish, which sea snakes like to eat!

LIONFISH

Lionfish are striped and have venomous spines lining their backs. When a mimic octopus fans its arms out around its body, it looks much like a toxic lionfish.

BANDED SOLE

Similar to flounder, soles are flat fish that live on the sandy bottom. A mimic octopus can flatten its arms alongside its body and slink along the seafloor, looking just like this poisonous fish.

RUNNER-UP
Veined Octopus

The veined octopus, also known as the coconut octopus, has a clever way of hiding from predators. It involves coconuts! The octopus grabs two halves of a coconut shell and pulls them close, then hides inside. Even if a predator spots the hiding place, it's hard to crack through the tough shell. Now that's an invertebrate who would win a game of hide-and-seek!

BIGGEST
Giant Pacific Octopus

Fast Fact!

Although this octopus lives only five years, that's actually pretty good for an octopus. Most octopuses don't live longer than a year. That means giant Pacific octopuses are the largest *and* the longest-lived of all the octopuses. Not too shabby!

THE GIANT PACIFIC OCTOPUS'S NAME says it all: These cephalopods are *big*. They're the largest of all the octopuses, growing to an average of 16 feet in length.

The biggest giant Pacific octopus ever recorded was even more impressive. It stretched to more than 30 feet long and weighed more than 600 pounds—heavier than a gorilla. Can you imagine running into that guy while swimming in the ocean? Talk about a real-life sea monster.

Giant Pacific octopuses live in—you guessed it—the Pacific Ocean. Although they're mostly found in shallower waters in the North Pacific, they're sometimes found in deep waters, too, up to 5,000 feet below the surface.

Despite their size, these octopuses don't live very long, only three to five years. That means they have to grow up quickly. They're one of the fastest-growing animals on the planet: They start as eggs about the size of a grain of rice and can grow to full size in just two to three years.

GIANT PACIFIC OCTOPUSES can eat large prey that other types of octopus can't handle, like big Dungeness crabs. They will also snack on fish, like this one, and even unsuspecting seabirds! Definitely not a cephalopod you want to mess with.

RUNNER-UP
Seven-Arm Octopus

Can you guess how the seven-arm octopus got its name? These cephalopods actually have eight arms, but males keep one arm hidden, so it looks like they have only seven. They are found in the deep sea, thousands of feet below the surface. They can grow to more than 13 feet long and weigh up to 165 pounds, making them the second-largest octopus in the world.

SMALLEST
Star-Sucker Pygmy Octopus

IF YOU'RE LOOKING FOR THE SMALLEST OCTOPUS in the sea, look no further than the star-sucker pygmy octopus.

Found in the shallow waters of the Indian and Pacific Oceans, the star-sucker pygmy octopus grows to a whopping total length of about 1¾ inches. Their mantle grows only to a half inch—smaller than a paper clip. They weigh as much as a stick of gum. In fact, full-grown star-sucker pygmy octopuses are smaller than the babies of some other octopus species!

Baby star-sucker pygmy octopuses spend their time drifting along with ocean currents before settling down on the seafloor as adults. We don't know a whole lot about these teeny critters, and we need to do more research to better understand their biology.

Scientists first described the star-sucker pygmy octopus in 1913, but more than 100 years later, we still have a lot to learn. Researchers think that their numbers are pretty healthy, but there have been only a handful of sightings (which is understandable . . . such a small animal would be easy to miss).

This is the **ACTUAL SIZE** of the star-sucker pygmy octopus!

RUNNER-UP
Southern Pygmy Squid

Although it isn't an octopus, the southern pygmy squid is worth mentioning because it is the smallest of all cephalopods. The males have a mantle only about ½ inch long—barely larger than the head of a thumbtack! Females grow slightly bigger, with their mantle stretching to about 1 inch—still shorter than a golf tee.

You might notice the star-sucker pygmy octopus and southern pygmy squid have similar names. In biology, sometimes the smaller species of different types of plants and animals have "pygmy" in the name, like the pygmy hippopotamus or the northern pygmy-owl.

COLDEST
Antarctic Octopuses

Fast Fact!

There have been octopuses in Antarctic waters for millions of years! Many deep-sea octopuses first evolved in the Antarctic, then moved to other ocean areas—all while staying in the cold, dark, deep sea.

THE WINNER OF THE "COLDEST OCTOPUS" AWARD actually goes to a group of octopuses: the Antarctic octopuses.

The Southern Ocean, which is the ocean surrounding Antarctica, is not an easy place to live. Water temperatures here range from about 28°F (–2°C), which is below freezing, to about 50°F (10°C).

We humans wouldn't last an hour in this freezing-cold water! But a number of species call the frigid waters of Antarctica home. There are even some that are **endemic** to this region, meaning they're found nowhere else in the world.

Things move a little slower in cold waters. Compared to octopuses that live in warmer habitats, Antarctic octopuses grow more slowly. In fact, the Charcot's octopus, which is found off the coast of Antarctica, has the slowest growth rate of any octopus.

MANY ANTARCTIC OCTOPUSES are in the genus *Pareledone*.

OCTOPUSES AREN'T THE ONLY CRITTERS THAT CALL ANTARCTICA HOME. Other Antarctic animals, like whales, penguins, and elephant seals, feed on octopuses and other cephalopods. On the flip side, Antarctic octopuses like to snack on small fish, worms, crustaceans, and more.

RUNNER-UP
North Atlantic Octopus

North Atlantic octopuses are found in the waters of the North Atlantic (surprise!) and Arctic Oceans. They like to live in deep waters where the temperatures hover just above freezing. They're not very big—weighing slightly more than half a pound—and as is the case for many deep-water species, there is much we still don't know about them.

Made for the Cold

Antarctic octopuses have a couple of cool adaptations that allow them to survive in such cold water.

- Their blue blood contains a special type of protein that helps them get enough oxygen in freezing waters.

- Their venom has unique toxins that can work in subzero temperatures. The venom from most other types of octopuses can't hold up in the cold!

People and
OCTOPUSES

From monsters and myths to science and technology

Gods, Myths, and Monsters

People like to tell stories about the things that surprise, inspire, and even scare them—including octopuses and other cephalopods. Here are a few examples of some of the most famous octopus tales through the ages, from around the world.

FIJI: According to Fijian lore, there was a fearsome shark god called Dakuwaqa who guarded the reefs near islands and rarely lost a battle. He met a big octopus and swam toward it with his mouth wide open. The octopus wrapped its arms around Dakuwaqa, squeezing until he begged for mercy. The octopus released him after Dakuwaqa promised to protect people from sharks when they went fishing—a promise that he still keeps.

JAPAN: The Ainu, an Indigenous people of northern Japan, tell stories of the terrifying Akkorokamui—a 400-foot-long red sea monster with huge eyes. The monster can supposedly grow back its own arms, just like octopuses can. If you are caught by the Akkorokamui, it's said, it's impossible to escape.

CARIBBEAN: According to Caribbean legend, the Lusca is an angry sea monster that lives deep in ocean caverns, called blue holes, in the Bahamas. It is said to grow to almost 100 feet. It also has long arms and can change color—sound familiar?

KIRIBATI: Na Kika is an octopus god of the Gilbert Islands, located in the Pacific island nation of Kiribati. Na Kika used his arms to help Riiki the eel separate the heavens from Earth. Legend has it that the octopus used to have 10 arms, but 2 of them were eaten by the hungry Riiki.

HAWAI'I: Kanaloa is a Hawaiian god symbolized by an octopus or squid. Kanaloa controls ocean winds, currents, groundwaters, and more, and also helps sailors navigate through the ocean's changing tides. He is one of the gods who helped create the world, and in some accounts, he created sorrow and other bitter things on Earth. There are other depictions of Kanaloa, under different names, throughout Polynesian myths.

SCANDINAVIA: One of the most famous mythical cephalopods is the Kraken: a massive, menacing monster who waits in the dark ocean for unsuspecting boats to come by. Thought to lurk off the coasts of Norway and Iceland, it's said to be the size of a small island. The Kraken has shown up in many TV shows, movies, games, and books.

Can you think of any other octopus stories? If you were to create a myth about octopuses, what would it be?

Real Scientists Studying Octopuses

Scientists all around the world are studying octopuses in labs, aquariums, and even at sea! Learning about these invertebrates and their relatives helps us understand their role in the ocean—and how we can protect them.

NAUTILUS

Expedition Octopus

With Megan Cook

Megan Cook has one of the coolest jobs on the planet. She works with Exploration Vessel *Nautilus*, a ship that travels the world answering questions about the ocean—including the deep sea! She's been on board for some *very* cool expeditions and seen plenty of cephalopods along the way. I talked to Megan about her adventures in the deep sea.

Q: Tell us about your job.

A: I am part of a team of explorers who create maps of the deep seafloor and drive giant car-size robots to explore the landscapes, animals, history, and makeup of our ocean. I help share all these discoveries with the world by inviting students onto the ship, streaming our discoveries live, and making videos online.

Q: What is your coolest octopus encounter?

A: We were on the last day of an expedition in the eastern Pacific, and the underwater robots were hustling to get to a small volcanic cone we wanted to survey. There wasn't much to see, just gray-brown sand. Then, all of a sudden, we saw the skeleton of a baleen whale covered with all kinds of scavenger animals. This little oasis of life, a **whale fall**, had small lobsterlike isopods, bone-eating worms, eelpout fish, and more than a dozen lavender octopuses snacking on it!

Q: What is it like living on a deep-sea research vessel?

A: Working on a ship is so fun and very hard work! A ship is like a little floating island with 51 people onboard. It takes lots of communication and teamwork. Living and working with all these fascinating people means I'm always learning! And the ship is constantly moving, so you get used to using handrails and bumping around a little while climbing in and out of bunk beds.

Q: What is the most rewarding part of your job?

A: Helping other people fall in love with the ocean! Plus, waking up every day with a 360-degree view of the ocean is always gorgeous!

Q: What is your favorite octopus species?

A: Dumbo octopuses! (*See page 44.*) I love that they are so many colors—orange, purple, white, pink! Why so many colors? I don't know! Obviously, I have lots more to learn.

You can see more from the E/V Nautilus *and Ocean Exploration Trust on their website. Check out the resources on page 69.*

These lavender octopuses are **CHOWING DOWN** on the remains of a baleen whale.

Studying Octopus Brains
With Dr. Z. Yan Wang

Dr. Z. Yan Wang is a professor who studies how animal brains affect their growth and behavior. She is a neuroethologist, meaning she looks closely at how animal brains are adapted for the lives they live. I interviewed her to learn more about her work with octopuses.

Q: **What are you researching about octopuses?**

A: Octopuses are so cool because their brains are really big and unique. That means we can ask all kinds of interesting questions about octopuses that we couldn't look at in other animals. I am really interested in how nervous systems change over long periods of time. (*To read more about the octopus nervous system, see page 16.*) I also look at how the brain changes over an animal's lifetime.

Q: **What does your typical day look like?**

A: We keep California two-spot octopuses in our lab, and mimicking their natural habitat and lifestyles is really important. Each day, we make sure the octopuses have good water quality, interesting activities, and a safe space for females to lay their eggs. Then we study the octopuses' brains and behavior at different stages—before, during, and after they lay their eggs.

Q: **We know octopuses don't live long after laying their eggs. Why is that?**

A: That's exactly what I'm studying! In vertebrates, animals that have bigger brains tend to live longer. Think about primates, whales, and elephants: They are big animals with big brains that live a long time.

Octopuses have really big brains for their body size. So why go through the trouble of developing a big brain if you don't live very long? It could be because older octopuses will eat the baby octopuses, which is bad for octopuses overall. It could be that mother octopuses live long enough to make sure their babies hatch, and then they die so they don't compete with the young octopuses.

Q: **What's the coolest thing you've learned in your research?**

A: We've known for a long time that there is a part of an octopus brain that cues the end of their lives. But through my research, we've learned that it's not just one cue—it's actually a rainbow of different factors at play. We see that the brain really lights up at the end stage of life.

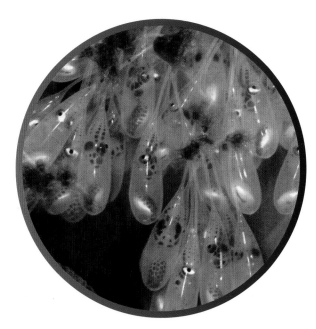

Dr. Wang studies why octopuses develop such *BIG BRAINS* but die so soon after laying eggs.

Q: **What is your favorite octopus species?**

A: I actually have a favorite individual octopus—there was a deep-sea octopus who brooded [took care of] her eggs for four and a half years! A deep-sea research expedition discovered her and was able to check up on her year after year. Stuff is happening in the deep sea all the time that we don't get to see, and here was an amazing example of humans encountering something completely unknown.

"Octopuses are so cool because their brains are really big and unique."

In the Lab
With Bret Grasse

Bret Grasse has worked with all kinds of cephalopods—from deep-sea octopuses to tiny cuttlefish and more. He is an expert in caring for cephalopods in places like aquariums and research centers. I talked to Bret about his job and some of his cool octopus encounters.

Q: Tell us about your job.

A: I have a really fun job: I work with octopuses, cuttlefish, squid, and nautiluses. They're very different from most animals, and I get to study and learn about them every day.

I provide animal care, like feeding them nutritious meals, taking care of them when they're sick, cleaning up their tanks, and interacting with them so they're happy and healthy.

Q: How do you decide what to feed the octopuses?

A: A lot of what we feed them in the lab is based on what they eat in the wild. We also get to know each specific animal. Some octopuses prefer crabs more than shrimp, and some prefer clams and mussels more than fish. When you work with them long enough, you essentially learn to "speak cephalopod"—you'll be able to see when they're excited, or if they don't like a certain food.

Q: What led you to study cephalopods?

A: They're basically the closest thing that we have to aliens on planet Earth. My first book report ever, in the third grade, was on octopuses. I've always been fascinated with them because they are so different from any other animal. They are truly bizarre.

Q: What do you love most about your job?

A: Sharing what I am passionate about with others, especially students, is a hugely rewarding part of the job. Also, one of my proudest accomplishments is being able to show rare, beautiful, and inspiring deep-sea cephalopods to the public for the first time.

Q: What's your favorite octopus?

A: That's easy: the blanket octopus (*page 43*). They're rare, they have this cool iridescent webbing, and the males are tiny and the females are huge! They can also steal the tentacles of box jellyfish and use them against predators.

The blanket octopus is
BRET'S FAVORITE!

"I think of cephalopods as the superheroes of the ocean because they have many superpowers: They have immense strength, they can shape-shift and change colors, and more."

OCTOPUS TECHNOLOGY

Octopuses' ability to shape-shift, change colors, trap prey, escape predators, and produce venom has excited scientists for years. What can we learn from octopuses, and how can we apply it to our own lives? Here are some ways octopuses have inspired new inventions.

Soft Robots

Picture a robot. You're probably thinking of a tall, stiff, metal robot that walks like a person, right? What if we could have robots that were less like the Tin Man from *The Wizard of Oz* and more like a soft, flexible octopus?

People around the world are using octopus-inspired robots that swim like cephalopods and help with underwater jobs. Scientists at Harvard even made an octopus robot that has no hard parts at all! The "octobot" moves on its own and can be made using a 3D printer. Next, they're working on octobots that can swim, crawl, and more.

Camouflage

Turning invisible is not just for superheroes! Octopuses use special cells in their skin to change their appearance to hide against corals, rocks, and the seafloor (see page 25). Scientists are trying to capture octopuses' camouflage skills with man-made materials that change color and shape against different backgrounds.

Bendy Surgery Tools

Octopuses' flexible arms can squeeze into tiny places and bend into odd shapes. This skill is perfect for doctors looking to do surgery on hard-to-reach places in our bodies. Don't worry, there aren't any octopuses in the doctor's office—scientists created a robotic arm that does the job instead. It acts like an octopus arm and can mean easier, safer surgeries for patients.

THIS OCTOPUS ARM SURGERY TOOL can move flexibly between delicate organs, represented here by water balloons.

Invention Time!

Let's put our thinking caps on. Brainstorm your own invention for each of the octopus features below!

- Radula (page 13)
- Mini brains (page 16)
- Venom (page 40)
- Cold-water blood (page 53)
- Ink (page 26)

Suction Cups

Octopus suckers are more than your average suction cup: They help octopuses climb, sense their environment, and handle objects (see page 15). Scientists in Virginia made a glove with suction cups inspired by octopus suckers on the fingertips.

The gloves have tiny light sensors in them that tell the suction cups to stick when they're close to an object—just like an octopus brain telling its suckers to grab something! These gloves can be used by scientists, engineers, and doctors who want to grab things in wet environments—including underwater.

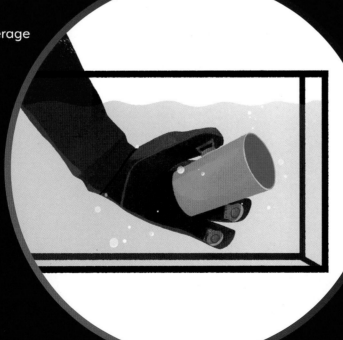

Keeping the Ocean (and Octopuses) Healthy

Humans are causing big changes in the ocean, which affects octopuses and all of the animals who call the ocean home. Fortunately, many species of octopus have healthy populations, so we're not worried about them going extinct. In fact, in some cases, octopus populations are increasing! There are many species, however, that we simply don't know enough about to tell whether they are doing well.

The best thing we can do for octopuses around the world is to keep our ocean healthy so that octopuses—and the habitats they depend on—can continue to thrive.

Cut Back on Trash

Humans make a lot of trash, and sometimes that trash ends up in the ocean. In fact, 12 million tons of plastic enter our ocean every year. Imagine swimming through a sea of plastic straws, bottles, bags, and string—yuck!

Scuba divers have seen baby octopuses hiding in piles of plastic trash on the ocean floor. Scientists have also discovered microplastics—tiny pieces of plastic—in octopus stomachs, which can be really bad for them! Trash leaks chemicals that can make octopuses stressed or even sick.

HOW TO HELP? No matter where you live, you can help keep trash out of the ocean. The best thing you can do is cut down on the amount of trash you make by reusing and recycling things when you can. You can also work with adults to clean up trash near streams, lakes, or beaches where you live. Just make sure to ask for help if you see something large or sharp.

We can all help keep our ocean clean, healthy, and safe for ocean animals, including octopuses.

Be Climate Friendly

For many years, humans have used fossil fuels like coal and gas to power our homes, cars, and businesses. When the gases released from those fuels are trapped in Earth's atmosphere, things can heat up. **Climate change** has meant that average temperatures on Earth—including in the ocean—are changing.

Temperature can affect how quickly octopuses hatch, how fast they grow, how much food they need to eat, and where they live. For example, as waters get warmer in Australia, the common Sydney octopus has started moving toward Antarctica in search of cooler, more comfortable temperatures.

HOW TO HELP? We can all make changes to cut down on our carbon footprint, like walking or biking instead of driving, turning off lights when we're not using them, and turning down the thermostat. You can also write to your local politicians to tell them why combating climate change is important to you!

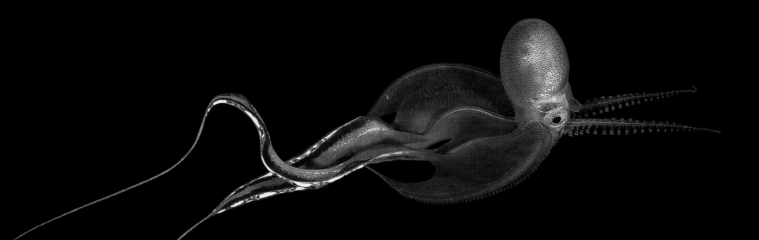

GLOSSARY

BIOLUMINESCENCE. When organisms make their own light

CAMOUFLAGE. When an organism's color or shape helps them blend in to their surroundings

CEPHALOPOD. A type of mollusk that includes octopus, squid, cuttlefish, and nautilus

CHROMATOPHORES. Tiny bags of color in octopus skin that help them camouflage

CLIMATE CHANGE. A significant change in Earth's average conditions over time

CUTTLEFISH. A cephalopod that is closely related to octopus, squid, and nautilus

ECOSYSTEM. All living organisms and nonliving physical features of an area

ENDEMIC. Found in only one particular place in the world

HABITAT. Area where an animal, plant, or other organism lives

HADAL ZONE. The deepest zone in the ocean

INTELLIGENCE. In animals, the ability to solve problems by learning about their environment

INVERTEBRATE. An animal without a backbone

IRIDOPHORES. Chromatophores that reflect light

MANTLE. A muscular sac that holds all of an octopus's organs

MELANIN. A dark pigment made in the bodies of animals and people that gives eyes, skin, hair, and octopus ink its color

MIMIC. To imitate the look or behavior of another organism

MOLLUSK. An animal in the phylum Mollusca, which includes snails, clams, octopuses, and more

NAUTILUS. A cephalopod that is closely related to octopus, cuttlefish, and squid

NERVE. Wirelike connections in the nervous system

NERVOUS SYSTEM. The brain, nerves, and other structures that work together to send messages around the body

NEURON. Nerve cells that carry messages through the nervous system

PAPILLAE. Skin bumps that can change shape and help an octopus camouflage

PIGMENT. A substance that adds color to something else

PREDATOR. An animal that lives by hunting other animals

PREY. An animal that is eaten by another animal

RADULA. A long strip with rows of teeth that helps octopuses eat their prey

REPRODUCTION. The process by which one or more organisms makes new organisms

SIPHON. A hollow tube on an octopus's body used for movement

SQUID. A cephalopod that is closely related to octopus, cuttlefish, and nautilus

SUCKER. A disk on an octopus arm that works like a suction cup and helps an octopus move and sense the world

TETRODOTOXIN: A deadly toxin found in blue-ringed octopuses as well as some fish and amphibians

TROPICS. Locations that are close to the equator

VENOMOUS. Describes an organism that inserts toxins into prey by biting or stinging

VERTEBRATE. An animal with a backbone

WHALE FALL. When a dead whale sinks to the bottom of the ocean and becomes food for others

GOING DEEPER

One of the best ways we can celebrate octopuses is by talking about them. Hopefully you can share the cool facts you learned from this book with your friends, family, and teachers! Plus, there are many more things to learn about octopuses. Check out all the books, websites, and other resources on this page.

Who knows what other octopus mysteries are waiting under the ocean waves? They're waiting for an explorer like YOU to uncover them!

All About Octopuses

SCIENCE FRIDAY: This fun and informative podcast is known for its deep dives into all kinds of scientific topics. Every year the producers release radio stories, articles, and videos about octopuses for Cephalopod Week! Fortunately, they compile these resources online to enjoy all year round.
https://sciencefriday.com/spotlights/cephalopod-week/

Celebrate Cephalopods

Don't miss the best week of the year . . . Cephalopod Week! Every year in June, aquariums, news sources, and others come together (virtually) to celebrate the stars of the invertebrate world. Keep an eye out for the summer event and search #CephalopodWeek on social media to find all kinds of fun posts about octopuses, squid, and more.

MONTEREY BAY AQUARIUM: You don't need to live near this California aquarium to enjoy it! Check out the cephalopod animal guide on the aquarium's website. There you'll find more about octopus anatomy and behavior, plus wallpapers for your computer, animal fact sheets, and quizzes.
https://montereybayaquarium.org/animals/animals-a-to-z/cephalopods

OCTONATION: Known as the world's largest octopus fan club, this website has enough octopus facts to occupy even the most dedicated cephalopod enthusiast. Explore different species in their Octopedia, then jump to OctoNation Kids to download a free workbook that has coloring sheets, games, and more.
https://octonation.com

Dive into Invertebrates

BRAINPOP: Put your knowledge from the book to the test! In the Sortify game, players group animals in bins based on what they have in common, like invertebrates, predators, and more. Try the games for invertebrates and for ocean life. Don't forget to reference the glossary on the opposite page to help with vocab!
https://brainpop.com/games/sortifyinvertebrates
https://brainpop.com/games/sortifyoceanlife

Explore the Ocean

OCEAN IMAGE BANK: Discover images from some of the world's greatest underwater photographers. These photos will take you under the waves to observe the spectacular habitats and wild creatures that call the ocean home—including octopuses. There are dozens of galleries and a search function to help you find exactly what you're looking for.
https://theoceanagency.org/ocean-image-bank

NATIONAL GEOGRAPHIC: Learn about ocean animals big and small with the massive animal database from National Geographic. You can search for specific animals, like the giant Pacific octopus and dumbo octopus, or browse collections of photos and stories of invertebrates, fish, and more.
https://nationalgeographic.com/animals/facts-pictures

OCEAN EXPLORATION TRUST (OET): Step aboard the deep-sea research vessel *E/V Nautilus* (and see page 59 to meet a scientist onboard). OET has a huge database of resources based on its deep-sea expeditions, including a 3D model of a whale fall covered in octopuses and a video of an octopus brooding ground. If the ship is at sea, you can watch in real time on the live stream.
https://nautiluslive.org

Help the Planet

NASA CLIMATE KIDS: Climate change is one of the largest threats facing our ocean today. The more we understand it, the better we can help combat it. NASA takes climate science and shares it in a clear, fun way through articles, games, and videos. Plus, you can learn more about the scientists studying our planet, from the depths of the ocean to outer space.
https://climatekids.nasa.gov

EPA'S PLANET PROTECTORS: The US Environmental Protection Agency (EPA) takes readers on a journey to save planet Earth. Your mission (if you accept it) will be to find a way to reduce waste and solve puzzles around trash and recycling. Booklets are printable and available in English and Spanish.
https://epa.gov/students/planet-protectors-activities-kids

Read More!

The facts in this book come from research papers and other books. Build your octopus library with these great reads.

Octopus: The Ocean's Intelligent Invertebrate
BY JENNIFER A. MATHER, ROLAND C. ANDERSON, AND JAMES B. WOOD
More advanced readers can take a deep dive into the biology and behavior of octopuses.

The Octopus Scientists
BY SY MONTGOMERY
Kids can follow along with real scientists as they study octopuses in French Polynesia. What will they discover? Adults and advanced readers will also enjoy Sy Montgomery's National Book Award finalist *The Soul of an Octopus*.

Octopus, Squid & Cuttlefish
BY ROGER HANLON, MIKE VECCHIONE, AND LOUISE ALLCOCK
While more advanced readers will expand their knowledge of octopuses and their relatives, everyone can enjoy the spectacular photos that fill each page.

For Educators

We cover a wide range of topics in this book, including octopus anatomy, behavior, species fun facts, and current research—and there is still more to explore! Check out our downloadable curriculum guide to learn how you can include the content in this book in your classroom. The guide includes suggested articles, videos, and activities that dive further into the wonderful world of octopuses. Activities target a range of age groups, are specifically designed to fit national science standards, and can be completed online or with materials found around the house. Find the guide at storey.com/the-incredible-octopus.

INDEX

Page numbers in *italics* indicate photos.

ACKNOWLEDGMENTS

Thank you to the incredible team at Storey Publishing, especially Hannah Fries, who believed in my dream of writing about octopuses and turned it into a reality. Thank you to Megan Cook, Dr. Z. Yan Wang, and Bret Grasse for sharing their stories of octopus research (and for answering all of my curious questions that didn't make it into the book). I am also grateful to my mentors throughout my academic career who have inspired my love of research—especially Dr. Jon Allen, who convinced me that invertebrates are actually the coolest.

Thank you to my family—the Spencers, Scheflows, and Baglinis—for raising me in a village of love, wonder, and deep appreciation of nature. Lastly, thank you to my husband, Corbin—you octopi my heart!